Tudors and Stuarts

Written by
Donna Cooper and Bill Cliftlands

Illustrated by
Vivien Monument, Steve Noon, Bob Venables

Designed by
Charlotte Crace

Edited by
Lisa Hyde

Picture research by
Helen Taylor

Picture consultant
Hazel Forsyth
Museum of London

CONTENTS

Tudors and Stuarts-who were they?

THE TUDORS

Henry VII was the first English king to come from the Tudor family. He became king after years of fighting, called the Wars of the Roses. The Tudor family tried to make the king the most powerful man in the land so there would be no more wars.

Henry VII's son, Henry VIII, married 6 times - each time hoping his wife would give him the son he needed to pass the throne on to. See pages 10-13 to see how this changed the lives of everyone in England.

Edward VI was Henry VIII's only son - but he died aged 15, after only 6 years as king.

1485   **1500**   **1515**   **1530**   **1545**

THE STUARTS

James I was the first English king to come from the Stuart family. He was already king of Scotland. He was Elizabeth's nearest relation. There was a very famous plot against James - we still mark this date every year with fireworks. Why? See pages 16-17.

Charles I was James' son. Charles argued with some of his people about who should rule the country. There was a war. How did this lead Charles to lose his head? See pages 20-21.

Charles II had tried to get the throne back after his father's execution. It took him 11 years. When he came back maypoles were set up all over the country. Why? See pages 20-21.

1603   **1615**   **1630**   **1645**   **1660**

Mary was Edward's sister. She was made queen when he died. But she died after being queen for just 5 years. She had no children, so her younger sister, Elizabeth, became queen.

Elizabeth I was one of the longest-reigning rulers we have ever had. She survived many plots against her, including a dangerous attack from Spain. Elizabeth did not marry or have children. When she died there were no more Tudor kings or queens.

1560   **1575**   **1590**   **1603**

James II became king after his brother Charles II died. He began to give a lot of the most important jobs to Catholics. The chief men in the country thought James was wrong and that he should no longer be king.

So they sent for James' daughter Mary. She was married to William of Orange, the Protestant ruler of Holland. They were made king and queen. James ran away to France. William and Mary had no children, so Mary's sister Anne became queen when they died.

Queen Anne was the last of the Stuart kings and queens - all of her children had died young.

1675   **1690**   **1705**   **1714**

The clues

History is a bit like being a detective. You find lots of clues from the past and then work out what might have happened. Historians call these clues **evidence**.

The evidence usually comes from **sources**. Sources can be written things - like diaries, letters, newspapers or books. Or sources can be **objects** - like pictures, buildings, furniture, tools and clothes.

Sometimes sources were written or made at the time you are finding out about - possibly hundreds of years ago. Sometimes sources were written a long time later - usually by other historians.

This book has a lot of sources - so how can you put the clues together for yourself? These two pages will show how you too can find out about Tudor and Stuart times.

These are the kitchens at Hampton Court palace. They are very big - so perhaps they had to feed a lot of people at once. There are no electric cookers on view - so how did they cook the food? The clue is the big opening in the wall on the left - it's a fireplace. So they seem to have cooked things over an open fire.

These are two large plates. The one above is plain wood. It was quite cheap and easy to make. The one below is made from pottery. A lot of work has gone into painting it. Which do you think cost more to buy? Which do you think was owned by a rich person?

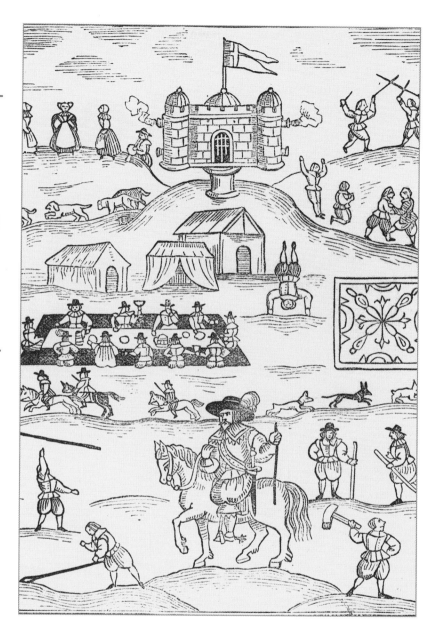

'Noblemen and gentlemen had hunting and horseracing. Ordinary people had the old Cotswold sports - wrestling, stick-fighting and shin-kicking.'

This is a picture of the Cotswold Games, which were held every year. People went there to have fun. They could watch the sports or join in.

The words at the top of the page are a source too. They were written by an historian, hundreds of years later. Can you see any of the sports he describes in the picture? The men are hunting on horses, and they have dogs. Where are the stick-fighters? What about the men who are shin-kicking? The pictures shows other things happening at the games, too. Can you see the acrobat? Some people are having a picnic - what's behind them? And look at the clothes they are wearing - do sportsmen dress like that now?

As you can see, you can get a lot of clues about what life was like in the past - just by looking at the evidence.

Now it's your turn!

Power

Tudor kings and queens could not rule England without help. So friends and important men stayed with them in their palaces. Often they became special officials. This was called the **Court**.

In the time before Henry VII came to the throne, England was often at war. The king was too weak, and some of the noblemen were too strong. Henry VII wanted to be the strongest man in the kingdom. He listened to advice from men in his Court - but he always made the final decision himself.

When Henry VIII became king he wanted to have time for more fun. So he had special friends called **favourites** to do more of the work for him. Thomas Cromwell was one favourite - he helped Henry get rid of his first wife, Catherine of Aragon (see page 10).

People wanted to be asked to Court. They wanted to be given **office** (a job), as they could be given money, land and a grand title. This would give them power.

RISE...

Cardinal Wolsey

Wolsey was only the son of a butcher - but he became Henry VIII's favourite. He became so rich he built Hampton Court Palace. Henry made him Lord Chancellor of England.

The Earl of Essex

Essex came to Court in 1587. He was young and handsome. Elizabeth made him one of her favourites. She gave him many offices - such as Master of the Horse and Earl Marshall. She also gave him a gift of £4,000.

AND FALL...

Cardinal Wolsey

He stopped being the king's favourite when he failed to end Henry's marriage to Catherine. He was ordered to the Tower of London - but he died on the way.

Earl of Essex - plotter!

The Earl of Essex was jealous of Robert Cecil. Cecil was also Elizabeth's favourite. Essex wanted to seize Whitehall Palace and get rid of Cecil. Essex was rebelling against the queen! He was found out and beheaded in 1601.

Court was not always fun!

Tudor courts were very rich and colourful to make the king and queen look wealthy and powerful.

Tudors also used paintings of themselves to make them look strong. Elizabeth got one artist to paint her looking her very best. Afterwards, most portraits were copied from this one. Artists who painted the queen in a different way could have their painting snatched from them!

See how this painting makes Elizabeth look great. What has Elizabeth got her hand on? How does her dress show that she was very wealthy? What can you see in the portrait to show she was queen?

Putting on a show

Tudor kings and queens also wanted to have fun at court. They wanted a lot of friends and servants with them. The court got bigger and bigger. Henry VIII had around 800 people with him - his daughter Elizabeth had 1500!

Henry VIII loved palaces. At first he had 12 - but he had 55 when he died. The palaces had to be very big for most of the court to live in. Hampton Court had 1,000 rooms with 280 beds.

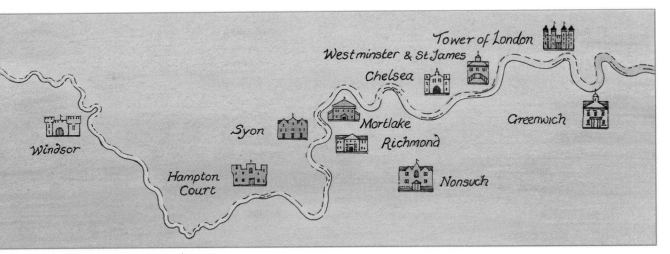

Roads were bad, so London palaces were always on or near a river. Boats would carry all the food and people.

It's a fact!
Greenwich Palace had a toilet so big that 28 people could sit on it at once!

Palaces were designed to be fun. Inside Greenwich Palace they had music and plays in big halls. Outdoors it had a park for hunting in, a tennis court and a bowling alley.

It's a fact!
In a year the court ate 8,200 sheep, 2,330 deer, 1,870 pigs and 1,240 oxen.

Food fact!
Queen Elizabeth ate sugar so often, her teeth went black.

Soup
Roast Lamb, Peahen,
Roasted Rabbits Chicken
Suckling Pig, Bacon,
Roast Veal,
Spiced Beef,
Roast Beef,
Baked Venison Tart,
Savoury Yorkshire Pudding

Here is a menu for a typical Tudor Court dinner. How much of this meal is meat? Is this healthy? What would you add to make it better?

Elizabeth I loved dancing - she was still dancing aged 69. Here she is dancing the Volta. Women were lifted so high you could see up their dresses - and women did not wear underclothes!

Food and fun were expensive. So Tudor kings and queens visited wealthy men and women at their homes in the countryside - to save money. They usually visited just once. Elizabeth visited the Cutte family twice and left them penniless!

Tournaments

Knights at court loved tournaments. That was when they went jousting. A joust was when two knights on horses charged each other with long poles called lances. A tournament was a colourful and exciting occasion. In 1595 the Duke of Cumberland entered a tournament riding a horse dressed like a dragon!

Henry VIII was a strong man. He loved to joust. In 1511 he held a special tournament at Westminster, to celebrate the birth of his baby son. You can see it in the picture below. Tournaments were held on other important days too, like Christmas.

Henry VIII

Henry VIII became king in 1509. He was born into the **Roman Catholic Church**. The Pope was the head of the church, and so Henry obeyed him. But by the time he died, Henry was head of a new **Protestant Church** without a Pope. How did this happen?

Henry VIII

Catherine of Aragon

Anne Boleyn

Boy or Girl?

Henry believed queens were weaker than kings. He thought that if his daughter Mary became queen when he died, war would ruin the country. People would die. So Henry wanted a son. His wife Catherine of Aragon could not give him one, so Henry had to ask the Pope to end his marriage. The Pope said no!

Henry was cross. He wanted to marry Anne Boleyn. She was having his baby - it might be a boy! Henry needed help. He called a Parliament to help pass a law making him the head of a new English Protestant Church. Henry did not need the Pope any more. He got his bishops (men who were high up in the Church) to give him his divorce instead. Henry could now marry Anne Boleyn.

Parliament

was a group of the most important men in the country. They met in a great hall in London. The king called a Parliament to give him advice and pass laws.

Why do you think the picture shows Henry VIII with his feet on the Pope's back?

Pull them down!

Protestants were people who did not like the Pope and the Catholic Church. They wanted to make it better - to reform it. They thought that priests in churches and abbots and monks in abbeys were greedy and bad. What do the two sources below say abbots and priests did that were wrong?

> *'Abbots and priests are greedy wolves. They have taken all the best farming lands.'*

A Protestant view on the Church in 1528

> *'The abbot of St. Edmundsbury Abbey gambled with dice and cards.'*

A report from the king's abbey inspectors in 1535

Historians now believe that Henry said abbots were greedy as an excuse to take their money. He wanted some of it to build castles to defend England from attack. So Henry closed the abbeys down. In two years he got gold and silver worth £7,000 and sold lands worth £29,000! He had the abbeys and nunnery buildings pulled down. Look at the picture above.

The ruins at Bylands Abbey

Rebellion!

30,000 Yorkshiremen were angry with the changes, and rebelled against them. They even put nuns back into the nunnery of St Clement's after they had been turned out. Why did people want the abbeys and nunneries open again? Find out from the sources below.

> *'The people in the North were poor. The abbeys gave them work.'*

Words spoken by a rebel leader

> *'In abbeys they had beer and bread.'*

A rebel song

God help us!

The Roman Catholic Church which Henry VIII tried to change was loved by most people. They were taught about God in church, and they went to christenings, weddings and burials there. Ordinary Catholics believed that prayers to God could stop terrible things like fires, plagues and floods.

God the farmer

Catholic farmers believed that God helped them on the farm. Priests prayed for rain to fall and sun to shine on the crops. Holy water was used to cure sick cattle.

Saints preserve us!

Saints were very good people who worked for God. Catholics thought that saints could cause miracles to help you if you prayed to them. St Roch cured the plague and St Apollonia cured toothache.

Most people couldn't read in Tudor England. They learnt about God from stories told in pictures, like the one below, not by reading the Bible.

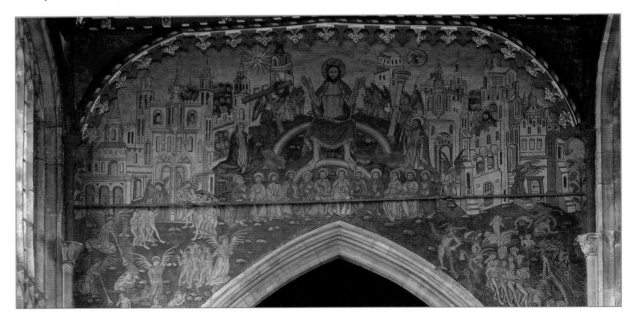

Relics

Churches liked to own parts of bodies of dead saints, or bits of their clothing - even something they'd used. People thought relics helped cure sickness and helped farmers. Men and women made long journeys to see the relics thinking that they would help them.

'At St Edmundsbury Abbey we found St Edmund's fingernail and St Thomas of Canterbury's penknife. We found skulls to cure headaches, and relics to cause rain and stop weeds.'

A letter from the king's men investigating abbeys, 1535

ALL CHANGE!

Protestants were glad the abbeys had gone, but wanted more changes.

Talking to God

Protestants believed that you shouldn't ask saints to talk to God for you - you should pray to God yourself. You couldn't ask saints for help with sickness or farming either. Now statues of saints were smashed and relics were burnt.

It's a fact!
The Bible used to be written in a very old foreign language called Latin. Most people couldn't understand it! Henry VIII had the Bible written in English so that people could learn how to be good.

A priest hole in Harvington Hall. The tiny hole the priest would have climbed through is in the top corner on the right. Can you see it?

Getting to Heaven

Protestants said only good people went to heaven. Reading the Bible was one way to learn to be good - listening to ministers' sermons was another. Puritans thought the best sermons were ones that lasted for hours!

Stop!

Catholics tried to stand up against the changes. Rich Catholics broke the law by inviting Catholic priests to give church services in their homes. If Protestants came to arrest the priests, they went into secret hideaways called 'priest holes'.

People in Devon and Cornwall were so upset that they even rebelled to get their old Catholic religion back.

Of wind and fire

Newsflash... 29 July 1588... England is in great danger. The most powerful country in Europe is about to invade.

In summer 1588, the Catholic king of Spain, Philip II, came up with a plan to conquer Protestant England. He was going to send an army and a huge fleet of 130 ships across the Channel. This was his **Armada**.

Many people expected Philip's plan to work. It didn't - and only half of his ships made it back to Spain. Why?

What's the plan?

Philip's navy was supposed to take his army over the Channel to England. The soldiers left from the Netherlands - the navy left from Spain. But no-one had worked out how they could talk to each other over long distances. So the navy didn't know where or when to pick up the army!

Fire!

When the Armada got close, the English set 8 of their own old ships on fire. Then they set them adrift. The Spanish were very scared when they saw the fireships coming towards them. They thought they were huge floating bombs called 'Hellburners'. So they escaped to sea as fast as possible. and didn't stop to pick up the army!

Bang!

The English guns were three times quicker to load and fire than the Spanish, as you can see from the written source below. They were also easier to aim. The Spanish cannon fired very heavy cannonballs which didn't travel as far as the English shot. Worse, Spanish cannon were so heavy, that when they were fired, they bounced back very hard. This sometimes damaged their own ships more than the English did!

'When we fire a cannon it takes us an hour to get it ready again.'

Written by a Spanish sailor a year after the Armada.

Shipshape!

Spanish ships weren't really built for this sort of fighting. They were old-fashioned compared to the English ones.

'The enemy's ships were very fast and nimble - so they could do whatever they wanted with them.'

Written by the Duke of Medina Sidonia, who was in charge of the Spanish fleet.

As you can see from the picture, Spanish ships were high at the front and back. This made them difficult to turn and sail. Can you see the difference in the two shapes - English ships weren't as high. They cut through the water easily and were quick to turn, as you can see from the written source above.

Wind!

There was a storm. All the ships were blown northwards. The Spanish decided that their ships were so badly damaged that they had better go home. They went the long way back - around the coast of Scotland and Ireland. Now there was a worse storm, and 25 ships were wrecked and over a thousand sailors were drowned in minutes.

It's a fact

The English thought God had sent the storms to stop the Armada.

An inside job?

Do you have fireworks on the Fifth of November? If you do then you are actually remembering something which happened nearly 400 years ago! It's called the **Gunpowder Plot** - and it's one of the biggest mysteries in history.

'Remember, remember
the Fifth of November.
Gunpowder, treason and plot!'

A nursery rhyme

Gunpowder

On 4 November 1605 Guy Fawkes was discovered in a cellar under the House of Lords. He was about to set light to 36 barrels of gunpowder. He'd been trying to blow up King James I and all the most important men in the government.

Fawkes was arrested and tortured. He said that other men had been working with him. The others were found. Some were killed trying to get away. The rest were tried and found guilty. They were hanged.

Fawkes' signature before and after torture. Why do they look so different? What difference would torture make to what Fawkes said?

Thumbscrews - a popular way to make people confess to crimes. How do you think they worked?

Treason

So why were they trying to blow up Parliament?

Fawkes and his friends were Catholics. King James and his ministers were Protestants. It looked as if the plotters were trying to get rid of the king, so that Catholics could take control of the country. One Catholic lord, Lord Mounteagle, had been sent a strange letter. It warned him to stay away from Parliament. But he passed the letter on to Robert Cecil, the king's most important minister. Soldiers were sent to search the buildings. They found Guy Fawkes.

At least, that is the story people have always believed. But the story is not that simple...

Plot

The Gunpowder Plot may have been helped by Robert Cecil himself! Why would he do such a thing? See if you can work it out from the clues.

The clues against Cecil

❧ Cecil was known to be worried about dangerous Catholics in England. A plot by Catholics would force the king to be harder on them.

❧ How did they get the gunpowder? All gunpowder was kept by the government. They stored it in the Tower of London. But the plotters managed to get hold of 36 barrels of gunpowder. Robert Cecil could easily get into the Tower. He was in charge of security.

❧ Who sent the warning letter? The mysterious letter was sent to Lord Mounteagle. Although he was a Catholic, everyone knew he was loyal to the king. Perhaps the letter was sent by Cecil. He knew that Mounteagle would tell the king, the plot would be discovered - and the Catholics would be in trouble!

This picture was drawn around the time of the Plot

War!

In 1642 King and Parliament were at war - against each other!

Parliament men were nicknamed Roundheads, the king's men Cavaliers.

War was dreadful. Father fought son and brother fought brother, if they chose different sides. What else was dreadful about war? Look at the sources below.

Cavalrymen - rode a horse, carried a pistol and a sword

The Royalists set fire to Birmingham

Soldiers paid for their own food and weapons out of their wages. So Parliament and the king had to raise new taxes (sums of money) to pay them. What else did the taxes pay for? The two written sources below show what an army would need to buy in order to live and fight.

'£5 to feed and cure Richard Hodgson. His nose was cut off and his leg broken, fighting in front of Greenhalgh Castle.'

An army payment, 1644

'The soldiers have not been paid and so they don't have enough clothes and other things. You must collect the tax of £200.'

A parliamentary order, 1647

Musketeers - carried a gun called a musket. A musket ball could go through armour!

Pikemen - carried a long stick or 'pike', which had an iron tip.

Siege

A garrison was a group of soldiers in a castle or big country house. People nearby paid taxes to the garrison so it would protect them. If people didn't pay up, the soldiers would steal their food.

Both sides tried to capture enemy garrisons. The parliamentary army surrounded Helmsley Castle in Yorkshire. It stopped soldiers inside from getting food. They had to surrender - they were starving. Parliament took down the gates and blew up a tower. No Cavaliers could defend it now!

Siege facts

Castle walls were three metres thick! Big cannons were needed. One Royalist cannon needed 70 horses to pull it!

Prisoners had no toilets. They were afraid they would be 'stunk to death'!

The tower at Helmsley Castle, blown up by Parliament

The New Model Army

The battle of Naseby was one of the most important battles that the King lost. Why did he lose? Parliament's 'New Model Army' had a lot of men who had fought before - so they were good at it. It was well paid, so men didn't run away. And it had brilliant officers like Oliver Cromwell. In 1646, the king finally gave himself up.

From 'Man of Blood' to 'Merry Monarch'

Newsflash... 30 January 1649... King Charles I has been beheaded outside Whitehall Palace.

The leaders of Parliament's Army were angry with Charles I. They blamed him for all the deaths during the civil wars. and so called him 'that man of blood'.

They wanted to bring him to trial. Oliver Cromwell, Parliament's most successful army general, soon agreed. Charles was found guilty and executed. A lot of people watched the execution. Was everyone happy that the king was dead?

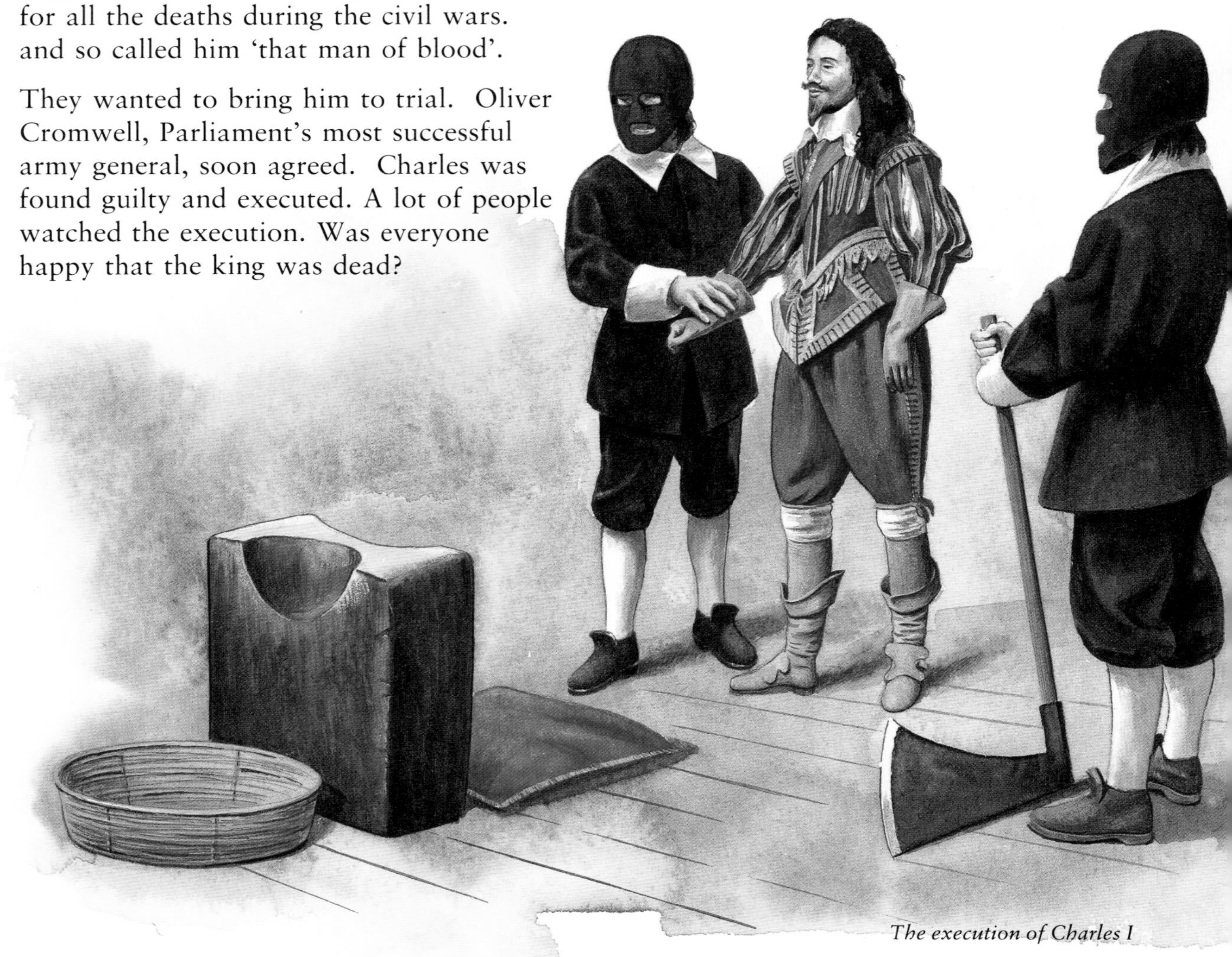

The execution of Charles I

'It was sad to see the axe fall. Thousands made the most terrible groan that I have ever heard.'

Written by someone at the execution

'Today it did not rain. But it was a wet day in London, because of all the tears that fell from many eyes.'

From a newspaper of the time

Oliver Cromwell and the Republic

England was called a Republic because there was no king. Now the most powerful man was Oliver Cromwell. But he too had his enemies, as you can see from the source below. He was a Puritan - a strict man who was very religious.

> ### 'A plague take Oliver Cromwell and the Devil rot his bones.'

Words reported to have been said in 1655

Life under Oliver Cromwell

Boring!

Cromwell passed laws making life boring. Many alehouses were closed. All acting was banned. Four actors from Richmond were 'whipped till their bodies be bloody' - just for acting! Worst of all - Christmas was stopped. People had to go to work instead!

Frightening!

People thought the army had become too powerful. In 1659 they even tried to rule England. People did not want to be ruled by people with swords and muskets.

The Restoration

Most people were fed up. They wanted to have a king again. What happened when people heard that Charles II was coming back? Look at the sources on the right.

People danced around maypoles again

> ### 'Great joy all yesterday in London. At night there were more bonfires than ever. Bells were rung and the King's health was drunk.'

Written by Samuel Pepys in his diary in 1660

Charles seemed to be more fun than Oliver Cromwell. He loved music, horseracing and the theatre.

No wonder he was known as the 'Merry Monarch'!

Hard times!

Today people who are old, or sick, or out of work are helped by the government. But the government in Henry VIII's time did quite the opposite! The sick and the old had to beg in the streets just to stop themselves from starving. Healthy men and women who didn't have a job were not allowed to beg. If they did, they were 'whipped until they bled'.

These sources show some of the ways beggars were punished. Do you think the punishments were fair?

The poor were badly treated, even though they couldn't help being poor. A family might have been left without wages when the father died. Some people were just too old to work.

So why were the early Tudor governments so hard on the poor? One reason was that they thought healthy people without jobs were just 'lazy'.

Sometimes there were suddenly more poor people around than usual. Like when the harvest failed, and lots of farm workers lost their jobs. At times like those, even more of the poor had to travel around in big gangs. Then the rich were scared of the poor - they thought they would be robbed.

But governments began to realise that some people couldn't help being poor. They still whipped and hanged people they thought were begging because they were too lazy to work, but they also

These men are in the stocks. Can you see how they worked?

found a way to help the others. They decided in 1572 that richer people should help to pay for the poor. Later, some of this money was spent on things like iron and flax, which the poor could be set to work on. This way the poor could earn their keep. An overseer of the poor was in charge of collecting the money from the rich and making sure it was spent properly.

An Abraham man

Didn't he do well!

One crank, Nicholas Gennings, made a small fortune as a beggar. He earned 70p a day at a time when labourers earned only 2.5p a day!

Wordplay

Beggars used special words so that they could talk to each other in secret.

Doxy - woman
Duds - clothes
Bouse - drink
Lightmans - daytime
Darkmans - nighttime

Try writing a secret message using as many of the beggars' own words as possible.

Nicholas Blunt 'the Upright Man' and Nicholas Gennings 'the Crank' were actually the same person! Why do you think he's dressed in two different ways?

Horsepower!

Mud! That's all most roads were made of. In winter people often couldn't use the roads because the mud was too deep. Roads weren't planned the way they are today, and they weren't built. They just 'happened' wherever enough people and horses had trodden a path through the grass. Roads were really only 'beaten tracks' - and they often shifted position! That's because people went off the 'beaten track' to find a dry bit to walk on.

Even in towns the streets were usually worse than today's farm tracks.

Travelling was hard. Most people walked everywhere. The furthest they went was to market. Richer people could travel by horse, so they could go longer distances.

'Most meat walked to market.'

This was written by a modern historian. What do you think it means?

These are pattens. What do you think they were for?

Some people did long-distance journeys in stage coaches. They were very slow and uncomfortable. Passengers usually felt 'car sick'. Coaches didn't even have windows until 1680.

Rolling along

By the end of Elizabeth I's reign, more people began to use coaches and waggons. By 1636 there were 6,000 coaches in London. Some were 'Hackney coaches' which were like taxis. The drivers were so bad that Hackney coaches were nicknamed 'Hackney Hell Carts'.

It's a fact
that James VI didn't find out he was king for 3 days after Elizabeth I's death. That was because it took so long to carry the message to Scotland. 3 days was thought to be very fast!

It's a fact
Queen Elizabeth's first coach was so uncomfortable she only used it once!

These were like today's long-distance lorries! They are packhorses. They carried goods from one end of the country to the other. Each packhorse could carry up to 125kg. But very heavy, bulky goods - like coal - went by water. Rivers and the sea were used much more than they are today.

This is a sedan chair - very popular with ladies in London. How do you think it worked?

Around the town

Towns changed during Tudor and Stuart times. Some got bigger and busier - with more houses and more people. But they were still dirty, dark and smelly.

Getting bigger

Towns like Norwich grew because the people there sold lots of cloth - so there were more shops, more traders and more poor people going there to get a job. The people needed homes, so gaps between houses were filled with new ones. The houses became cramped together. This happened to other towns too - look at the picture below.

Shops in Chester today - in Tudor times the most important shops were just on the top floor.

Southwark in London. Can you see any gardens?

Rubbish!

There was no rubbish collection like today. What we flush down the toilet, people then just threw out of their windows! Others threw their filth into rivers and ditches. This made people sick - because they took their drinking water from them!

A tight squeeze!

Streets were very narrow because they had been made when most people walked and carried goods in barrows. Now lots of coaches and carts sped along them, hitting customers and shops, so the most important shops were built one storey above the road.

Towns were busy. Can you see any evidence of this in the written source below?

'In every street, carts and coaches make a noise like thunder. Hammers are beating. Salesmen skip from one shop to another..'

A writer on London in 1606

Towns then were different to today's towns in other ways. The written source below shows some of them - what are they?

'In some towns the countryside could be seen from most streets. There were barns. Colchester had farmland in it.'

A modern historian

Houses and shops

Poor labourers lived in houses with just one or two rooms. Some rich London merchants had 14 or 15 rooms built on 5 floors! Many people lived over their shops. Their window-shutters opened downwards and became shop counters.

Tradesmen often ran out of space for their goods. One London coal dealer had sacks of coal in her bedroom!

Market towns

Market towns had large, open spaces called market places. Farmers went to market to sell their goods and buy things like cattle or corn. Can you find the corn market in the map below?

Nottingham

Nottingham was a market town. It had 60 different kinds of worker - but leather was its main business. Tanners made leather out of the skins of animals - like cows and pigs (called swine). Can you find the 2 places with animal names in the map below? Glovers and shoemakers then turned leather into things people could wear.

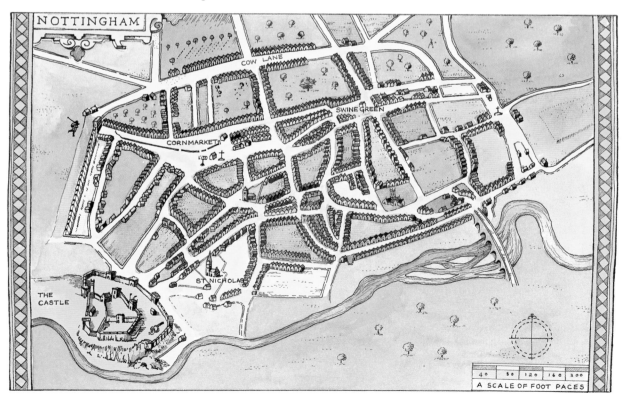

What important buildings can you see in this map of Nottingham?

In the country

Most people lived in small villages - not in towns. Nearly everyone worked on farms. But others were craftsmen, like blacksmiths and carpenters, who helped farmers by making horseshoes and ploughs. Most people had to work very hard just to feed themselves.

Labourers

A lot of the hardest work was done by labourers. They were paid just 1 or 2p a day. They worked very long hours - often starting work at 5 o'clock in the morning. Labourers lived in huts with just one or two rooms. They had no chairs - and often no tables. Labourers were so poor they had no change of clothes to wear.

The Hall

Sometimes there was a huge house or Hall owned by the rich lord of the village. He owned most of the land. Poorer farmers gave him money (or even grain or animals) so that he would let them farm some of his land.

Open Fields

Villagers farmed narrow strips of land. They were scattered across 3 big fields in the village. Two of the fields would be used for growing wheat, barley or oats. But the third field would be left fallow - that meant the field would be left alone for the year, so the soil could rest. Then it would grow better crops the next year.

The Common

This was open land that no-one owned. All the villagers could use it - but the poor needed it most. They put their few sheep and cows on it to eat the grass. They also got wood from the common for fuel.

The Church

People learnt about God at church (see pages 12-13). But people also went there to see friends and have a gossip. Farmers and craftsmen did business in the churchyard.

Women

Most women worked very hard in the country. There were no supermarkets, of course - so farmers' wives had to bake their own bread, brew the beer, grow the vegetables, make the cheese and butter, and collect eggs from the hens they kept. They also cooked the family's meals and looked after the children.

The Alehouse

People went there to drink, sing and meet their friends. (See page 31)

Yeomen

Yeomen owned or rented big farms. Many of them were getting richer in Elizabeth's reign - because they improved their land. Their homes got bigger and better - with more rooms, chimneys, and glass in the windows. More were now built in stone. Yeomen did not sleep with the cattle as poorer people did!

Fun and games

Tudors and Stuarts did not work the whole time. Sometimes they went to alehouses, to drink and sing with their friends. On special days, like May Day, they played games and did sports.

Play the game

We still play some of their games today, like Hide and Seek. They played bowls on village greens. And whole villages played football against each other. It was very different from today's game, as you can see from the written sources below.

'There were few rules, no lines, and any number could join in.'

Written by a modern historian

'Football is more like a friendly fight than a game! Sometimes necks are broken - or backs, legs or arms. Noses gush with blood.'

Written by a Puritan, 1583

Some games we don't play today, like cudgel-play, where the idea was to hit your opponent with a wooden stick until he bled!

Holiday!

The Catholic Church had special days called 'Holy Days'. People didn't have to work on Holy Days - so they became today's 'holidays'! On Shrove Tuesday there were lots of football matches. At Christmas people danced, sang and ate mince pies.

Some holidays were very special for farmers - like May Day. Then people were happy to see the crops growing again after the winter, so they had fun and games. There were morris dancers and maypoles.

Sometimes crowds gathered for lots of different sports. These events were called 'Games', such as the Cotswold Games. Noblemen and gentlemen came from as far as 60 miles away! So what did people do at the Cotswold Games? See the picture opposite.

The Puritans didn't like people getting drunk.

Drink Up!

Ale (or beer) was drunk a lot in Tudor times, because there wasn't any tea or coffee. But an 'Ale' was also the name of a party with lots of beer! So a 'church ale' was a party to collect money to mend the church. A 'cuckoo ale' was held when people heard the first cuckoo in Spring. What do you think 'bride ales' and 'Midsummer ales' were held for?

Puritans hated alehouses, and they hated too much singing and dancing too. Why do you think Puritans hated church ales? Look at these two written sources.

The Cotswold games

On the stage

People loved watching plays. But the first theatre wasn't built until 1576! Before that, plays were put on in market places, in the yards of big inns - or even in the homes of rich people. Some wealthy people actually kept their own group of actors.

One of the most famous groups of actors was the 'Lord Chamberlain's Men'. King James I liked them so much he took them over, making them the 'King's Men' One of them is very famous today - William Shakespeare. He wrote plays for them. The plays were so good we still perform them today - 400 years later! Another member of the King's Men was Richard Burbage. He was the star of many of Shakespeare's plays. Burbage's father built the very first proper theatre.

It's a fact!
The first proper theatre was just called 'The Theatre'.

'The Theatre' was pulled down in 1598. It was moved plank by plank to a new site! It was rebuilt and given a new name - 'The Globe'. Some of Shakespeare's greatest plays were seen here for the first time, there is a picture of it below.

The Globe had 24 sides, so it looked like a wooden 'O'.

The building came to a nasty end, when a special effect went wrong during a play. The thatched roof was set on fire and the theatre burned down in just 2 hours.

William Shakespeare

The picture of the inside of the Swan theatre which you can see on page 33, was drawn in 1590. It's the only picture we have of the inside of an Elizabethan theatre. But there are problems with using this as evidence.

First, it's not a very good drawing, and the details aren't clear. Second, this is only a picture of the Swan theatre - other theatres may have looked quite different!

Inside out!

The centre was open to the sky, so there were no plays in rainy weather. There was no lighting either so plays had to be put on in daylight.

A flag flew when a play was about to start.

The most expensive seats were those in the gallery behind the stage. The gallery was used for some bits of the play too.

Up to 3,000 people squeezed into the theatre. Some were in the 3 galleries. Some sat on the edge of the stage.

Doors on stage led to the dressing rooms.

For a penny the audience could stand around the stage. It was noisy, cramped and smelly.

There were no female actors in Shakespeare's time. The women's parts were played by men or boys!

There was a trapdoor in the stage, so ghosts, witches and devils could 'magically' appear!

Childsplay?

Children in Tudor and Stuart times worked very hard. Poor children could be sent out to work when they were only 6 years old. Their families needed the money.

If their parents made cloth, then the children might have to wash wool all day. On a farm the children would work in the fields. Some jobs were so tiring that girls working as servants thought they were the lucky ones!

Craftsmen usually taught their sons how to do their own job. So a tailor was probably the son of a tailor too. Sometimes children were sent to live with another family to learn a different craft. This was called **apprenticeship**. The boy had to stay with the new family for 7 years. He wasn't paid, but he did get his food and clothes.

This baby is 6 months old! What differences can you see between the way it is dressed and the way we dress babies today?

'Elizabethans thought of children as small but troublesome adults.'

Written by a modern historian

Children did have some time for playing. Can you work out which of these toys belonged to rich children? Look at the toy musket. What do you think happened to it?

Spinning tops and balls.

A hard lesson?

Tudors thought it was very important that children should have lessons - especially boys. Lots of new schools were built during this time. They were called grammar schools. The pupils usually came from wealthy families, but sometimes poorer boys went too.

It's a fact!

In some schools boys had to speak in Latin all day - even at playtime!

It's a fact!

Elizabethan boys often started school at 6 o'clock in the morning!

It's a fact!

History wasn't taught in schools!!

This is a grammar school in 1592. How many rooms did it have? What happened to naughty boys? The big boys have books, but the smaller boys are using hornbooks like this one above. Can you tell what hornbooks were for?

Newsflash... 19 September 1665... Over 7,000 Londoners have died of the Great Plague this week. Over 100,000 people in London will probably have died by the end of the year.

The illness called plague wasn't a new thing for London. There were outbreaks nearly every summer. In 1625 over 40,000 people had died of plague. 1665 was even worse.

In 1665 no one knew the real causes of plague. But people did have their own ideas. Some thought plague was caught by touching plague victims, others by breathing in 'bad air' and others by magic! All the sources on these two pages show things people did so they wouldn't catch the plague.

These men carried away the bodies of plague victims. They usually smoked pipes.

'ABRACADABRA was written on charms worn by people who hoped it would keep the evil away!'

A modern historian

'One doctor, George Thomson, worked with a dead toad hanging around his neck!'

A modern historian

'The coaches and waggons are full of people escaping to the countryside.'

Samuel Pepys wrote this in his diary on 21 June 1665

> **'Watchmen, who have to keep watch over the houses of plague victims, must make sure that no one goes into the house and that no one comes out.'**

This was an order made by the Lord Mayor of London in 1665

> **'Anyone going outdoors should put amber oil on their nostrils.'**

A doctor's advice

A doctor's outfit.

Bitten

The real cause of the Great Plague was a germ spread by fleas like the one below. The fleas usually lived on rats, but sometimes the fleas bit people. Then the germ would get into the victim's blood. They would begin to feel very ill. These are the symptoms the doctor would look for:

Headache
Sickness
High temperature
Lumps in the armpits and at the tops of the legs. (These lumps are called buboes - which gives the disease its name, bubonic plague.)

A quarter of the victims got better at this stage. BUT if black spots and a rash appeared, then the victim would probably die within a few days.

Actual size

It's a fact!
Plague still exists in some parts of the world today.

Fire!

Newsflash... 2 September 1666... A huge fire has started at the king's baker's in Pudding Lane in London.

The Great Fire of London lasted for four days. It was dreadful. By the time it had been put out, four-fifths of the City had burned to the ground. Over 100,000 were left homeless. Yet only eight had died. Work out why the fire spread so quickly by looking at the written sources.

'The wind was very high and going in the direction of the City. We have had no rain for so long that even stone churches burn easily.'

Written by Pepys on 2 September 1666

'The houses are packed close together. They are full of things that burn easily. And there are warehouses full of oil'

Written by Samuel Pepys in his diary on 2 September 1666

'... the noise and crackling of the fire, the screaming of women and children, the falling towers, houses and churches.'

Written by John Evelyn who saw the Fire

In Tudor and Stuart times there were big fires in many towns - not just London. Most towns had houses like these. How many fire risks can you see in this picture? What are they?

Put it out

Leather buckets held water. They weren't much help in big fires.

This woodcut was made at the time of another big fire - at Tiverton in 1612

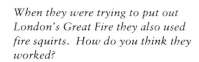

When they were trying to put out London's Great Fire they also used fire squirts. How do you think they worked?

It's a fact!
The king helped fight the Great Fire

Fire hooks were very useful. They were used to pull down buildings. That made a fire break - a gap in a row of buildings which is too big for the fire to leap over. It stops the fire spreading. Gunpowder was sometimes used to blow up houses to make wider fire breaks.

Out of the ashes

The Fire burned down:
13,200 houses
88 churches
44 halls
and 3 prisons

After the Fire the City had to be rebuilt. The Government ordered it to be in brick and stone! One very famous new building was St Paul's Cathedral. It was one of 52 new churches designed by just one man - Sir Christopher Wren.

Watch it!

You probably have science lessons at school - but 400 years ago people knew very little about science. But in Stuart times, a few men started to look carefully at things, to see how they worked. They began to do tests - or **experiments** to prove their new ideas about how things worked. These men were scientists.

King Charles II was very interested in science. He even did some experiments himself! He was so excited by the scientists' work, he gave his support to the club where they discussed their new ideas. Now it was called the Royal Society.

Galileo

> ***'The King has been present at many of the Society's experiments. He's also helped with them.'***

Written by Thomas Sprat in 1667

> ***'The moon is not smooth. It's rough and full of holes and bumps like the surface of the Earth.'***

Written by Galileo in 1610

Two new inventions meant that scientists could see things no one had ever seen before...

Looking up!

People could now see things like planets which were very far away - by looking through a **telescope**. A famous Italian scientist called Galileo used a telescope in 1609 to watch the stars and planets. Now he could see distant stars which had been invisible before. And for the first time, he could prove that the Earth and other planets move around the Sun.

Using his telescope, Galileo could see the surface of the moon well enough to draw it.

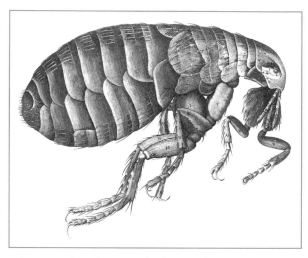

This is Hooke's drawing of a flea. Without a microscope the flea would look about as big as full-stop! Look at all the details he could now see clearly.

A great English scientist, Isaac Newton, invented an even better telescope which gave a much clearer picture. Many modern giant telescopes are still based on Newton's own tiny telescope.

Close up

Scientists could also see much smaller things than ever before - by looking through a **microscope**. This made tiny things look bigger.

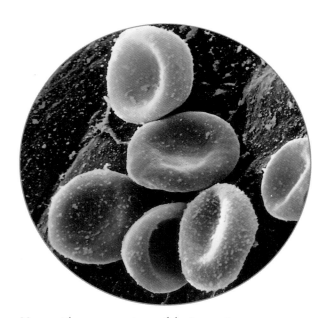

Now, with new, more powerful microscopes we can see things that were invisible to people in Stuart times - like this blood cell.

Robert Hooke was an English scientist who made lots of drawings of very tiny creatures by using a microscope like this one.

The invention of the telescope and microscope were very important. They have helped scientists ever since. We have been able to discover more and more about how the world around us works, how living things are made, what causes illness and what's deep in space.

Witches?

At Halloween we pretend to be witches - but people in Tudor and Stuart times actually believed in them! They thought that 'witch magic' could hurt people - but that it could help them too.

Help!

In Tudor and Stuart times there were no doctors for people to go to when they were sick. And there were no policemen to help them when things were stolen. The new Protestant church wouldn't let people pray to saints for help any more. So some people went to white witches instead. White witches cured sicknesses with herbs (often the same herbs today's doctors make medicines from). And they helped find stolen goods by asking questions - just like policemen do today.

Nowadays we would not say that the witches were magic - we would say that they were very clever.

Black magic

People thought that some witches were bad because they had evil powers given to them by the Devil. They could hurt, or even kill, people just by touching or staring at them. To see what people thought witches did look at the written source.

Two witches and their imps.

> ## 'People said that witches killed or hurt farm animals, and stopped cows from giving milk.'

Written by a modern historian

How to spot a witch!

People believed that a witch had a spot on her body that would not bleed if you stuck a needle in it. People also believed witches and wizards had a little devil or imp with them. They thought the imps were sometimes shaped like cats! Look at the picture opposite -what other animal shapes could they have?

Why were people called witches?

Some men and women who were very poor were called witches by richer people. Old women were the poorest in the village, and so they were often called witches.

How it happened

An old woman who was hungry asked a rich neighbour for food. When the neighbour said no, the old woman got angry. She would then wish that something awful would happen to the family. Later, if the rich person's child or animal got sick, they would say the old woman had caused it. She was a witch!

Proof?

Of course, people actually fell sick because of germs - not a witch's curse! But Tudors and Stuarts often blamed witches. People thought they had a way to prove that someone was a witch. This was called 'swimming'. Look at the picture below. A poor woman has been dropped in water. Her hands and feet were tied together. If she floated, she was a witch. If she sank, she was not. What do you think could happen if she sank? Was this a fair way to test for a witch?

A big new world

For hundreds of years sailors had been trying to find an easier way to get to China, India and the Spice Islands - the East. The East was where merchants from Europe bought furs, silks, jewels and spices - then they sold them again at home. They made a fortune. Explorers knew the world was probably round, like a ball. So they thought that if they sailed westwards and just kept going, they would finally end up in the East.

But there were two problems with this idea. First, the world was a lot smaller than they thought. Second, there was a huge continent in their way - and they didn't know it!

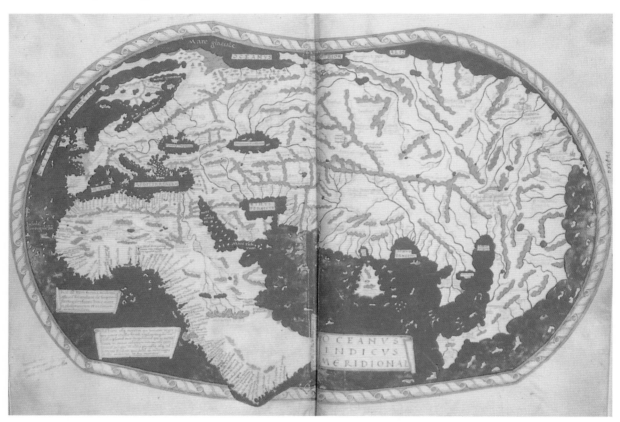

Christopher Columbus discovered the new land by accident in 1492. He thought he'd found the Indies, but he was wrong. It was only in 1507 that Amerigo Vespucci worked out that it was a new continent. It was America.

It opened out a whole new world for merchants. And that's exactly what they called it - the New World.

This map of the world was made about 1489, a few years after Henry VII came to the throne. Europe is on the left, Africa is at the bottom and China is on the far right. Compare it with a school atlas - can you see what's missing here?

Fed Up!

Imagine a world without crisps, chocolate and cornflakes. They are just three things we wouldn't have today if America hadn't been discovered. They are made from plants which once only grew in America - the potato, the cacao tree and sweetcorn. The explorers also brought back pineapples and tomatoes - but no one in England would eat them. They thought they were poisonous!

Up in smoke!

Tobacco was a plant found in America. The Indians who lived there before the Europeans arrived smoked the weed in clay pipes. The English soon took up the awful habit.

> ### 'The Indians think smoking tobacco is so good that even their gods love it.'

Written by Thomas Hariot who went on expeditions with Sir Walter Raleigh. He was probably the first Englishman to die from smoking.

Do you think this man's family like his new habit?

> ### 'Tobacco makes men's insides like a kitchen. It dirties them with an oily soot.'

Written by King James I. Possibly the first government health warning!

It's a fact

When Sir Walter Raleigh persuaded Queen Elizabeth to try a puff, people thought he was trying to poison her!

Scuppered!

The Mary Rose stayed
hidden in mud at the
bottom of the water for
over 400 years. But in the
1970s a group of people
called **archaeologists**
decided to explore its
remains. It was a
wonderful chance to find
out about Tudor ships and
the men who lived on
them. They wanted to
find out how the Mary
Rose had sunk.

*This painting of the Mary Rose was
on a list of Henry VIII's ships and
their equipment. The list was made
about the time the Mary Rose sank.*

*Archaeologists managed to lift the
remains of the Mary Rose out of the
water. They looked at them carefully
and measured them, so they could
work out how the ship would have
looked before it sank. They had a
surprise - the Mary Rose turned out
to be very different to the painting.
How many differences can you see?*

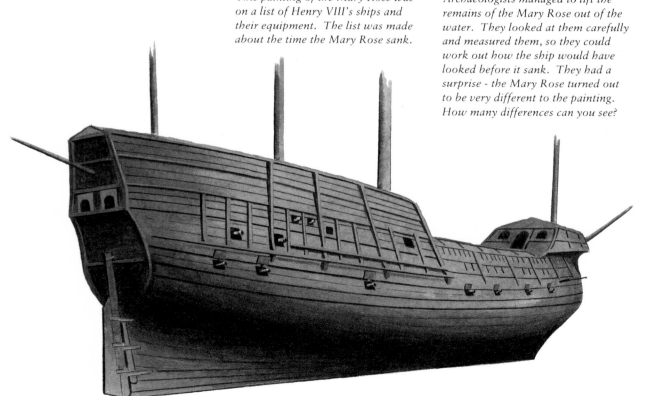

All aboard!

Thousands of things that the sailors would have used every day were found on or near the wreck. The mud had kept them in a very good condition as you can see from the sources. The Mary Rose was a fighting ship. Do you think the men on board had any spare time? If they did, how did they spend it?

A backgammon set found in the carpenter's cabin.

'The leather covers of books and several dice were found.'

Written by people who worked on the Mary Rose wreck.

Musical instruments found on the wreck.

How do you think the men ate on the Mary Rose? Were they all treated the same? What would make their diet healthier?

3 kg 175g biscuits	170g butter
32 litres beer	340g cheese
3 kg 625g salt beef	
350g fish	

A sailor's weekly rations in 1565

Officers probably ate from pewter dishes like the ones above. Who do you think used dishes like the ones below?

It's a dog's life

One of the men kept a pet dog on board. It's skeleton was found near the bones of a rat it had probably been chasing!

Index

Numbers in **bold** *indicate illustrations*

Published by BBC Educational Publishing, a division of BBC Education, Woodlands, 80 Wood Lane, London W12 0TT

First published 1993

Paperback ISBN: 0 563 35376 7
Hardback ISBN: 0 563 35377 5

Colour reproduction by Daylight, Singapore
Cover origination by Goodfellow & Egan, Cambridge
Printed and bound by BPCC, Paulton

Photo Credits
Archiv für Kurst und Geschichte **p. 40 (top)**; Reproduced by permission of the Marquess of Bath, Longleat House, Warminster, Wiltshire **p. 34 (top)**; Archdiocese of Birmingham/Harvington Hall **p. 13**; The Bridgeman Art Library/Private Collection **p. 7**; The British Library **pp. 26 (left)** *Maps 175.t.1.(4) detail*, **32 (left)** *G7884, The Theatre of the Empire of Great Britain by John Speed (1611)*, **44** *Add 15760 ff 68 verso - 69*; The College of Arms **p. 9 (bottom)** *The Westminster Tournament Roll*; Reproduced by permission of Viscount De L'Isle, from his private collection **p. 9 (top)**; Devon Library Services/Focus Photography **p. 39 (top right)**; English Heritage **pp. 11, 19**; Mary Evans Picture Library **pp. 10, 18, 21, 33, 36, 45**; Fotomas Index **p. 23 (right)**; Crown Copyright. Historic Royal Palaces/Photographer Earl Beesley **p. 4 (right)**; Michael Holford **p. 41 (left)**; Hulton Deutsch Collection **pp. 5, 16, 17, 31, 35, 42**; Master and Fellows, Magdalene College, Cambridge **p. 46**; Mansell Collection **p. 22 (top right)**; The Market Harborough Museum, Leicestershire Museums, Arts and Records Services **p. 34 (bottom)**; The Mary Rose Trust **p. 47**; Museum of London/Photographer Torla Evans **pp. 4 (left), 24, 34 (middle), 39 (left and bottom right)**; National Portrait Gallery, London **p. 32 (left)**; Photo-Leisure Photographic Agency/Michael Reed **p. 26 (right)**; Royal Commission on the Historical Monuments of England Crown Copyright **p. 12**; The Science Museum **p. 40 (bottom)**; The Science Photo Library **p. 41 (bottom right)**; Wellcome Centre for Medical Science **pp. 37, 41 (top right)**.
Front cover: National Portrait Gallery, London **(left)** *Elizabeth I by unknown artist*; Board of Trustees of the National Museums and Galleries on Merseyside (Walker Art Gallery, Liverpool) **(right)** *Charles II by Sir Godfrey Kneller.*